Typewriter Poems
ed: Peter Finch

something else press /
second aeon publications

This book is published in the u.k. by second aeon publications,
3 maplewood court, maplewood avenue, cardiff cf4 2nb, wales.

The following International Standard Book Numbers apply to this
title:

      0-87110-078-9   (u.s. edition)
      901068 26 8   (u.k. edition)

contents

preface to u.s. edition

From its beginnings, concrete poetry has had a special relationship with the typewriter, due to the simple fact that all typewriter characters on a given machine (certain electric models excepted) are of equal width, which opens up vast graphic possibilities. The review *material* (1957-1960) in Darmstadt, Germany was completely set on typewriters, Olivettis being the preferred make. During the 1960's, with the so called "mimeograph revolution" the possibilities were explored further in many lands, from India to Canada, the United States to Czechoslovakie, Sweden to Uruguay.

Some of the most interesting work in this typewriter genre within the general medium of concrete poetry was and is being produced in the United Kingdom. And since one of the most interesting of serious magazine editors is *Second Aeon's* Peter Finch, he was in a position to make up one of the most exciting collections. The ultimate, universal collection it is not - it makes no pretense at internationalism. But a constellation from an epicenter of the whole concrete earthquake it is. And it's in that spirit that we are proud to present it.

The Publisher

Introduction

Typewriter: An Instrument for writing by means of type, a typewheel, or the like, in which the operator makes use of a sort of keyboard, in order to obtain impressions of the characters upon paper.

Webster's international dictionary, 1907.

in this age all poets use typewriters. some just copy their manuscripts for the benefit of clarity, others have slightly more graphic ideas behind their thumpings. this is a collection of work from those others.

in some poetry there is rhythm, and there is rhyme, there is a metrical structure within which the poet expounds his ideas, spends his words. its hard work. in typewriter poetry there is no rhythm, and there is no rhyme, but there is a metrical structure. the space bar, the ratcheted roller, the keys themselves. within those limits the poet explodes his ideas, burns his words. its not easy either. some poets are more structurally minded than others - they add and adapt the basic meter. coloured ribbons, masks, different pressures, overlaps.

gerard manley hopkins wasn't the only holy man to make ingenious
use of meter - sylvester isn't bad either.

it is difficult to tell quite what makes a typewriter poem (or type-
stract as edwin morgan named them) - what makes them *typewriter*
poems rather than just concrete or experimental texts. (a few ass-
orted definitions will be found in the notes at the end of this book).
the consensus of opinion seems to be that the peculiarities of the
typewriters' spacing itself pinpoints the difference, ie: a typestract
works when done on a typewriter but fails when re-set in printers
type. the letters "a", "m", "i", & "l" for example, all occupy the
same space on a typewriter but all differ in printers type.

the majority of works in this collection tend to be typestracts in the
fullest sense, others to a slightly lesser degree. they represent the
work of almost every typewriter poet of significance at present
working in the u.k. from bob cobbing's vast duplicator overlays and
dsh's olivetti masterpieces to cavan mccarthy's simple but effective
structures.

arabesques, lawrence pedersen calls them. but they are often more
than that. visual structures built for amplification by voice and extem-
porization by feet - cobbing's sonic icons, paula claire's performance
pieces, andrew lloyd's sound sequences. all typewriter poems, all
human but impossible without the machine.

peter finch

                    the beg
              the word and th
           ne thing that is called
          though thus beings immeasurab
         word was with god and the word
          tao is elusive evasive evasive elusive
        innumerable and   unlimited are   eman
        was god the same was in the beginning
        et latent in it are forms elusive evasi
        there are in reality   no beings that are
        with god all things are made by him and
        et latent in it are objects dark and dim
        ever emancipated   why   subhuti if   a bodhisa
        without him is   not anything made   that w
        et latent in it is   the life force the l
         retains   the thought of an ego a   persona
         made   in him was life and the life was
          force being   very   true latent in it ar
           being or a soul he is no more a bo
             the light of men and the   light s
            evidences from   the   days of old
            again   subhuti   then   a   bodhisa
              in the darkness and the
               now its named   have r
                 practises   chari

thomas a. clark   a cosmos

7

an

anna

annalife

annalifey

annaliffey

annalivia

annalive

anna

na

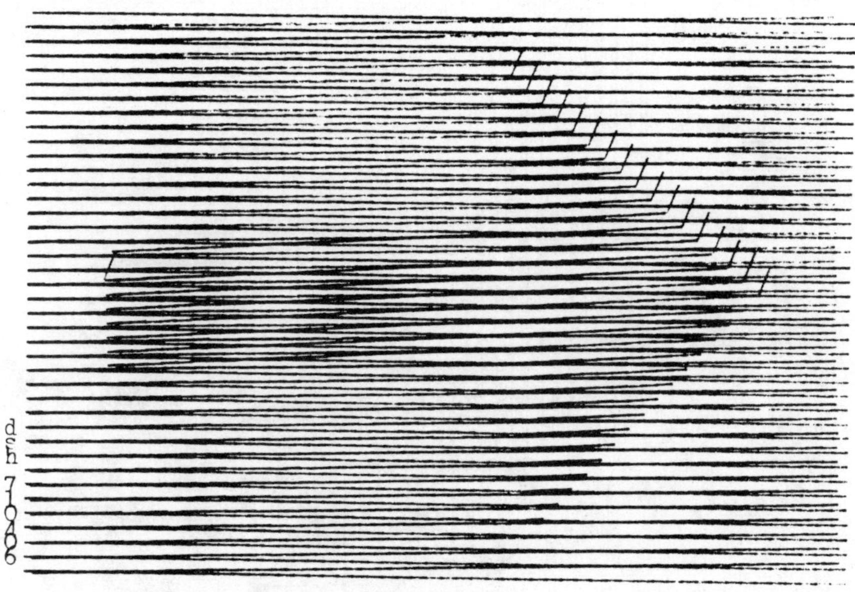

dsh

above: untitled
page 10: from the welsh aedoeology
page 11: garden ornamonument to volapuk

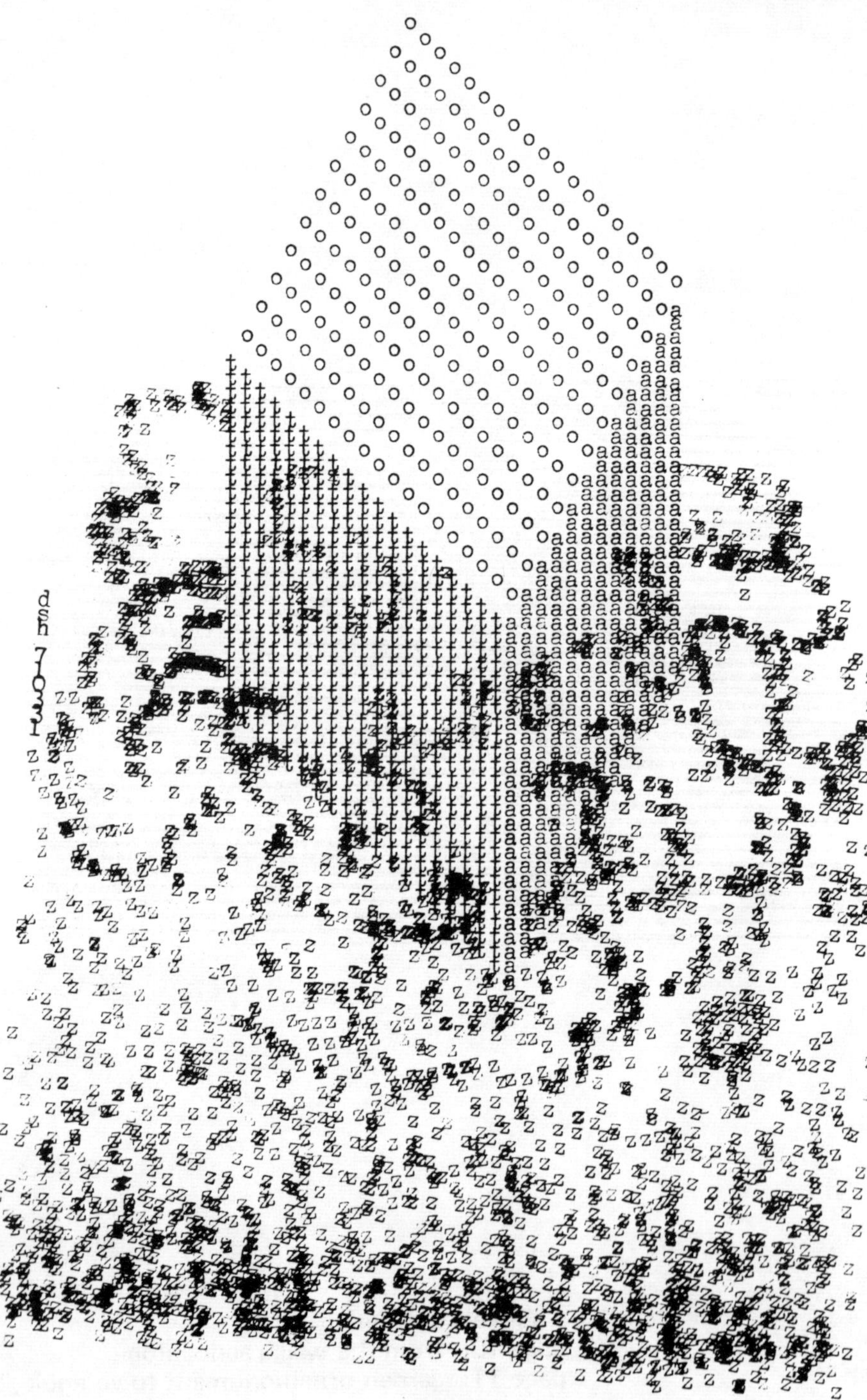

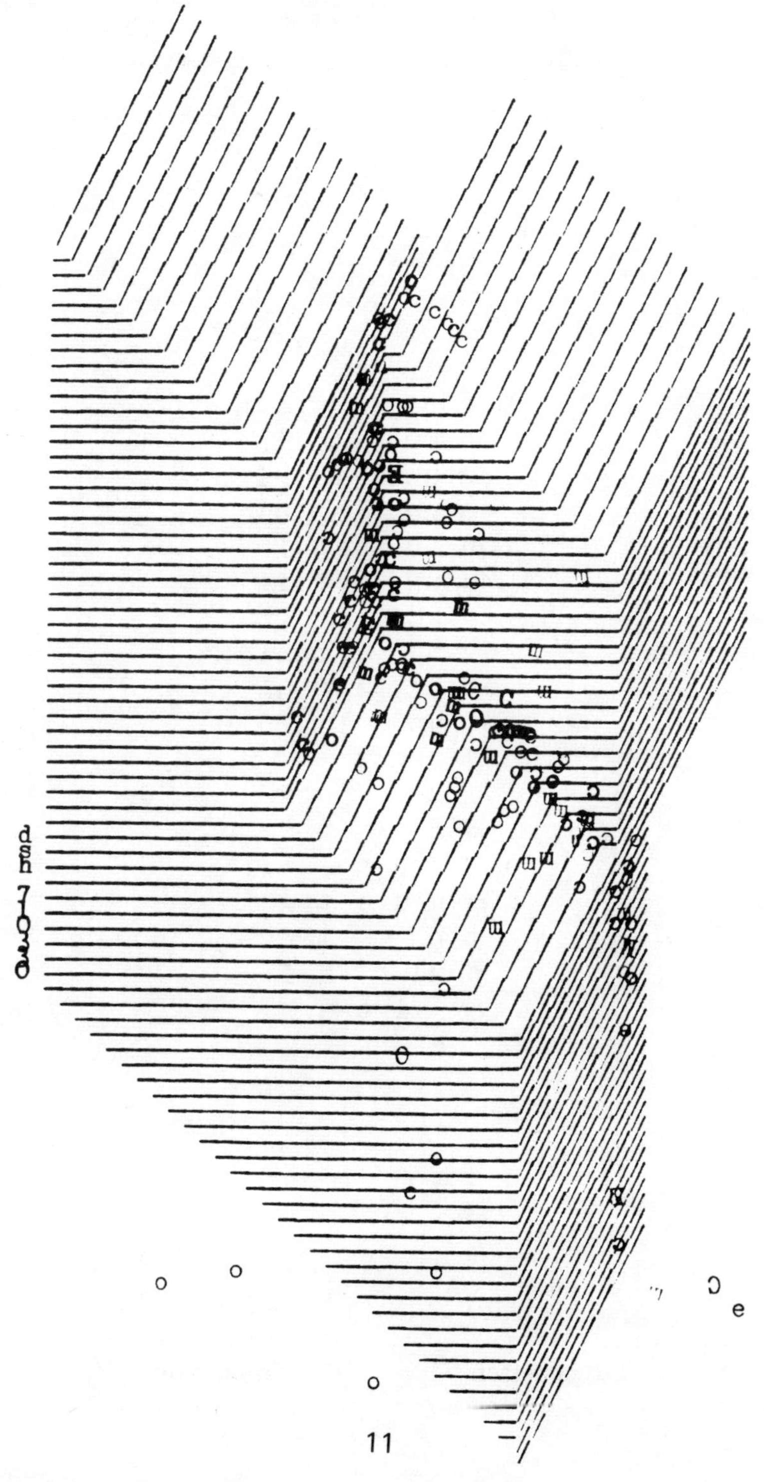

```
m o u n t a i n
 mo un    ta in
 om un    ta ni
 om nu    at ni
 mo nu    at in
 no un    at in
 mo nu    at in
 om nu    at ni
 om un    ta ni
 mo un    ta in
n    n t       n
  o u      a i
   m n      t n
o     u a       i
o m n u a t n i
  m n      t n
  o u      a i
  a   i o u
     e
```

l.d. pedersen   mountain

badbadbadbadbadbadbadbad
badbadbadbadgadbadbadbad
badbadbadbadgodbadbadbad
badbadbadbadgoobadbadbad
badbadbadbadgoodadbadbad
badbadbadbadgoodgdbadbad
badbadbadbodgoodgdbadbad
badbadbadoodgoodgdbadbad
badbadbagoodgoodgdbadbad
badbadbagoodgoodgobadbad
badbadbagoodgoodgooadbad
badbadbagoodgoodgooddbad
badbadbdgoodgoodgooddbad
badbadodgoodgoodgooddbad
badbaoodgoodgoodgooddbad
badbgoodgoodgoodgooddbad
baddgoodgoodgoodgooddbad
baddgoodgoodgoodgoodgbad
baddgoodgoodgoodgoodgoad
baddgoodgoodgoodgoodgood
baodgoodgoodgoodgoodgood
boodgoodgoodgoodgoodgood
goodgoodgoodgoodgoodgood

fffffffffffffffffffffffffffffffffffffff   s s s s   fffffffffffffffff
                                          s s s s
                                       s s s s
                                    s s s s
                                 s s s s
                              s s s s
eeeeeeeeeeeeee   s s s s   eeeeeeeeeeeeeeeeeeeeeeeeeeeeeeeeeeeeee
                  s s s s
               s s s s
            s s s s
bb   s s s s   bbbbbbbbbbbbbbbbbbbbbbbbbbbbbbbbbbbbbbbbbbbbbbbbbbbbbbbb
bbbbbbbbbbbbbbbbbbbbbbbbbbbbbbbbbbbbbbbbbbbbbbbbbbbbbb   s s s s   bb
lllllllllllllllllllllllllllllllllllll   s s s s   lllllllll
                                                s s s s
                                             s s s s
                                          s s s s
                                       s s s s
ooooooooooooooooooooooooooo   s s s s   oooooooooooooooooooooo
                                s s s s
                             s s s s
                          s s s s
                       s s s s
wwwwwww   s s s s   wwwwwwwwwwwwwwwwwwwwwwwwwwwwwwwwwwwwwwwwwwwwwwwwwwww

andrew lloyd   tidal poem (ebbs & flows)   , no's 1-4.

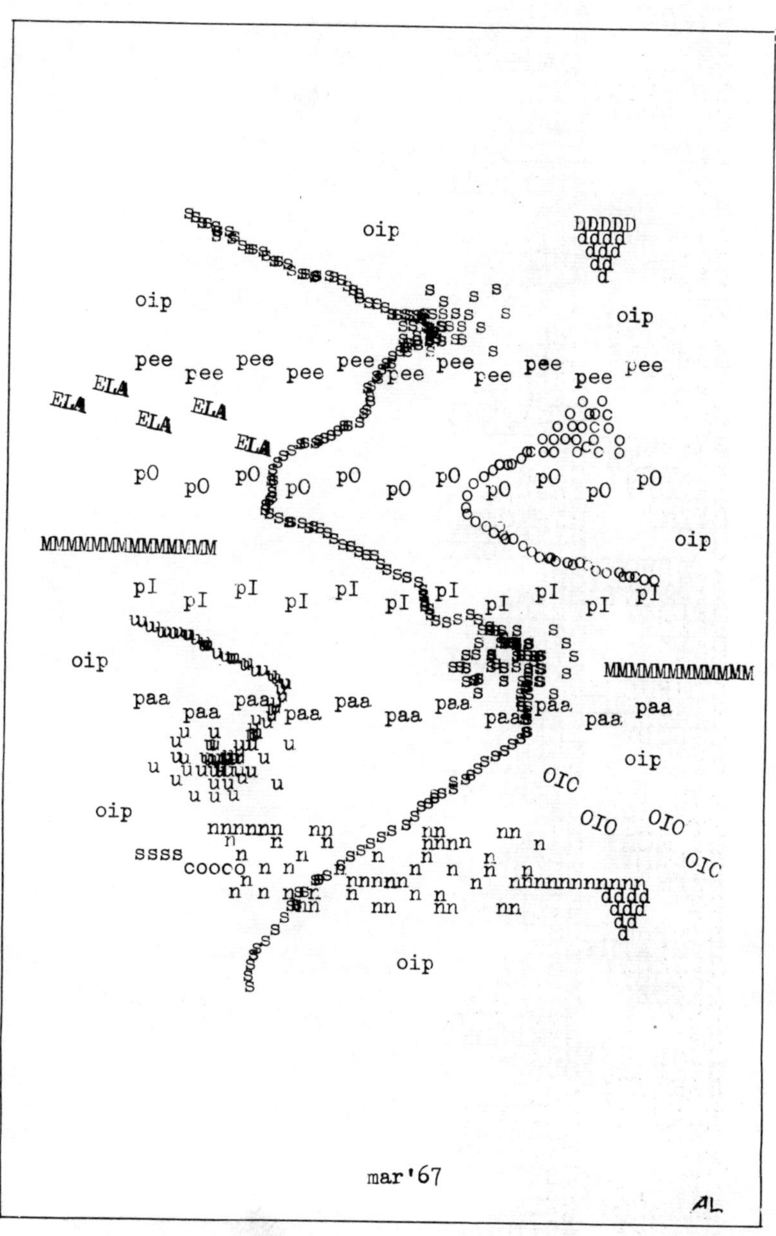

andrew lloyd   **5th dolphin transmission**

15

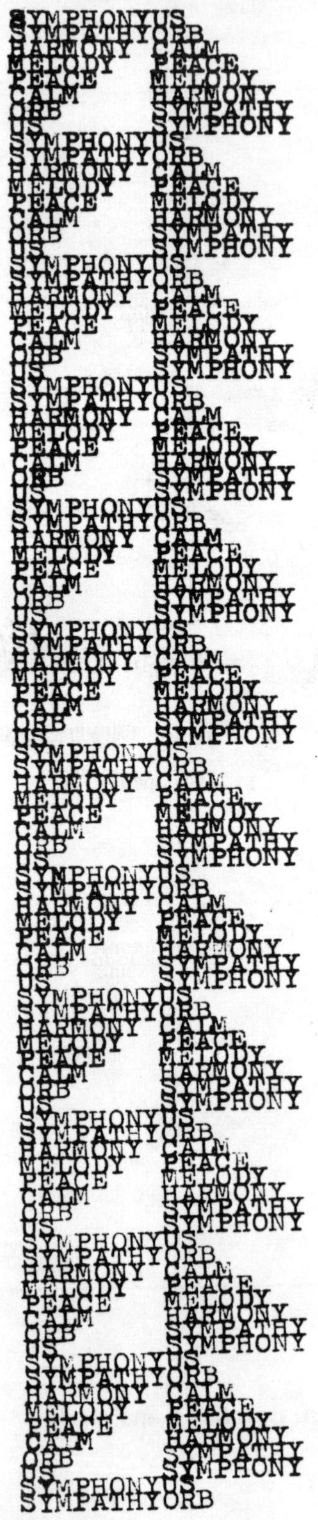

paula claire

epithalamion

right: weld

16

john gilbert   eve

```
        o                   n                   a
       pos                 ons                 fan
      xposu               const               ofani
     exposur             econsti             nofanim
    eexposure           reconstit           onofanima
   heexposurea        dreconstitu         ionofanimag
  theexposureandreconstitutionofanimage
   heexposurea        dreconstitu         ionofanimag
    eexposure           reconstit           onofanima
     exposur             econsti             nofanim
      xposu               const               ofani
       pos                 ons                 fan
        o                   n                   a
       p  s               o   s               f   n
      x    u             c     t             o     i
     e      r           e       i           n       m
    e        r         r         t         o         a
   h          d       a           u       i           g
  t            n     n             t     o             e
   h          d       a           u       i           g
    e        r         r           t       o         a
     e      r           e           i       n       m
      x    u             c           t       o     i
       p  s               o   s               f   n
        o                   n                   a
       pos                 ons                 fan
      xposu               const               ofani
     exposur             econsti             nofanim
    eexposure           reconstit           onofanima
   heexposurea        dreconstitu         ionofanimag
  theexposureandreconstitutionofanimage
   heexposurea        dreconstitu         ionofanimag
    cexposure           reconstit           onofanima
     exposur             econsti             nofanim
      xposu               const               ofani
       pos                 ons                 fan
        o                   n                   a
```

alan riddell   hologrammer

i i i i i i i i i i i i i i i i i i i i i i i i i i i i i i i i
i i i i i i i i i i i i i i u i i i i i i i i i i i i i i i i i
i i i i i i i i i i i i i u u u i i i i i i i i i i i i i i i i
i i i i i i i i i i i i u u u u u i i i i i i i i i i i i i i i
i i i i i i i i i i i u u u u u u u i i i i i i i i i i i i i i
i i i i i i i i i i u u u u u u u u u i i i i i i i i i i i i i
i i i i i i i i i u u u u u u u u u u u i i i i i i i i i i i i
i i i i i i i i u u u u u u u u u u u u u i i i i i i i i i i i
i i i i i i i u u u u u u u u u u u u u u u u i i i i i i i i i i
i i i i i i u u u u u u u u u u u u u u u u u u u i i i i i i i i
i i i i i u u u u u u u u u u u u u u u u u u u u u u i i i i i i
i i i i u u u u u u u u u u u u u u u u u u u u u u u u u i i i i
i i i u u u u u u u u u u u u u u u u u u u u u u u u u u u u i i
i i u u u u u u u u u u u u u u u u u u u u u u u u u u u u u i i
i u u u u u u u u u u u u u u u u u u u u u u u u u u u u u u u i
i i u u u u u u u u u u u u u u u u u u u u u u u u u u u u u i i
i i i u u u u u u u u u u u u u u u u u u u u u u u u u u u u i i
i i i i u u u u u u u u u u u u u u u u u u u u u u u u u i i i i
i i i i i u u u u u u u u u u u u u u u u u u u u u u i i i i i i
i i i i i i u u u u u u u u u u u u u u u u u u u i i i i i i i i
i i i i i i i u u u u u u u u u u u u u u u u i i i i i i i i i i
i i i i i i i i u u u u u u u u u u u u u i i i i i i i i i i i
i i i i i i i i i u u u u u u u u u u u i i i i i i i i i i i i
i i i i i i i i i i u u u u u u u u u i i i i i i i i i i i i i
i i i i i i i i i i i u u u u u u u i i i i i i i i i i i i i i
i i i i i i i i i i i i u u u u u i i i i i i i i i i i i i i i
i i i i i i i i i i i i i u u u i i i i i i i i i i i i i i i i
i i i i i i i i i i i i i i u i i i i i i i i i i i i i i i i i
i i i i i i i i i i i i i i i i i i i i i i i i i i i i i i i i

alan riddell   **the affair**

b

b

b

b

b

b

b

b

b b b b

b b

b b

b

b b

b b b

b

b b b

b

b b

b b

b b b b

b b b b

b b b b b

b b b b

b b b b b

b b

b b

b b

b

b

b

alan riddell   the honey pot

```
        y         e c h                       o e           y
y       y         e c h           a d               e d d   y       a i
y n     y                         a d   y     o e d                g a i
    n   y     d e c h     e u a d     y r             d d          g a i
    n   y         e c h r e               r   o e d d d   y       g
    n         d e c                                   d                 a
y n     y                                             d d         g
y       y     d e c h r                 y     o e d       y
y n     y             e u a d                 o
              d   c h r e u   d     y r   o e                             r
y n     y         e c h           y r         e d       y       a i r
y n     y     d e   h r e u a     y r   o   d d           g             r
    n             e c h     a d     r   o             y             i
    n         d e     r e   a d     r   o e d d   y   g               r
y n     y     d     h               r             d d           a i r
        y         e c h     a d               e d               a
y n               r e u a d                         d d         g       r
y       y                     a             e d       y           i r
y n     y         c h             d     r             d d   y         i r
    n   y     e c h     u a d     r   o       d           g       i
        y     c                         o e d d                       r
y                 e c h     a d                 d d         g a
y n               c h     a d     r                                 i r
y n     y   d e c                       o                           a
    n         d e c                 y r       d d   y               r
              c h         d   y r     e           y   g
```

meic stephens

genesis

FREEDOM
REEDOMF
EEDOMFR
EDOMFRE
DOMFREE
OMFREED
MFREEDO
FREEDOR
REEDORH
EEDORHY
EDORHYD
FORHYDD
ORHYDDI
RHYDDID

meic stephens

osmosis

mauve   mauve   mauve   mauve   mauve   mauve   mauve
mauve   mauve   mauve   mauve   mauve   mauve   mauve
mauve   mauve   mauve   mauve   mauve   mauve   mauve
mauve   mauve   mauve   mauve   mauve   mauve   mauve
mauve   mauvemauvemauvemauvemauvemauve   mauve
mauve   mauvemauvemauvemauvemauvemauve   mauve
mauve   mauvemauvemauvemauvemauvemauve   mauve
mauve   mauvemauvemauvemauvemauvemauve   mauve
mauve   mauvemauvemauvemauvemauvemauve   mauve
mauve   mauvemauvemauvemauvemauvemauve   mauve
mauve   mauvemauvemauvemauvemauvemauve   mauve
mauve   mauvemauvemauvemauvemauvemauve   mauve
mauve   mauvemauvemauvemauvemauvemauve   mauve
mauve   mauvemauvemauvemauvemauvemauve   mauve
mauve   mauvemauvemauvemauvemauvemauve   mauve
mauve   mauvemauvemauvemauvemauvemauve   mauve
mauve   mauvemauvemauvemauvemauvemauve   mauve
mauve   mauvemauvemauvemauvemauvemauve   mauve
mauve   mauve   mauve   mauve   mauve   mauve   mauve
mauve   mauve   mauve   mauve   mauve   mauve   mauve
mauve   mauve   mauve   mauve   mauve   mauve   mauve
mauve   mauve   mauve   mauve   mauve   mauve   mauve
mauve   mauve   mauve   mauve   mauve   mauve   mauve
mauve   mauve   mauve   mauve   mauve   mauve
         mauve   mauve   mauve   mauve   mauve
mauve   mauve   mauve   mauve   mauve   mauve   mauve
         mauve   mauve   mauve   mauve   mauve
mauve   mauve   mauve   mauve   mauve   mauve   mauve
mauve   mauve   mauve   mauve   mauve   mauve   mauve
mauve   mauve   mauve   mauve   mauve   mauve   mauve
mauve   mauve   mauve   mauve   mauve   mauve   mauve

philip jenkins   purple; study 3 : for mark rothko

nadanadanadanadanadanadanadanadanada
nadanadanadanadanadanadanadanadanada
dadadadada
nadanadanadanadanadanadanadanadanada
dadadadadadada
nadanadanadanadanadanadanadanadanada
dadadadadadadada
nadanadanadanadanadanadanadanadanada
dadadadadadadadada
nadanadanadanadanadanadanadanadanada
adadadadadadadadada
nadanadanadanadanac   adanadanada
adadadadadadadadada
nadanadanadanadada   danadanada
dadadadadadadadadada
nadanadanadanana   anadanada
dadadadadadadadadada
nadanadanadada   nadanada
dadadadadadadadadada
nadanadanadan   nadanada
adadadadadadadadadada
nadanadanad   anadanada
dadadadadadadadadadada
nadanadana   nadanada
dadadadadadadadadadada
nadanadanac   anadanada
dadadadadadadadadadada
nadanadan   nadaanada
dadadadadadadadadadada
nadanadada   nadanadana
dadadadadadadadadadada
nadanadanad   anadanadana
dadadadadadadadadadada
nadanadanada   adanadanada
dadadadadadadadadada
nadanadanadanac   nadanadanada
dadadadadadadadadad
nadanadanadanada   adanadanadanada
dadadadadadadadadad
nadanadanadanadan anadanadanadanada
dadadadadadadadada
nadanadanadanadanadanadanadanadanada
dadadadadadadadada
nadanadanadanadanadanadanadanadanada
dadadadadadadadad
nadanadanadanadanadanadanadanadanada
dadadadadadadadada
nadanadanadanadanadanadanadanadanada
dadadadadadadada
nadanadanadanadanadanadanadanadanada
dadadadadadadada
nadanadanadanadanadanadanadanadanada
dadadadadadada
nadanadanadanadanadanadanadanadanada
dadadadada
nadanadanadanadanadanadanadanadanada

```
love head eyes bawl bend wake feet wink soap
come yell nose soul rest tell wash poop bath
rose kiss look bell days howl wind sulk talc
baby rusk lips arms mole neck back tail talk
hand hold room gaze want wall tale seat mama
          blue bird purr burp dada
          toys crib pram tree walk
          milk suck pins grin pink
          hair pond bark crow wish
          dogs wait mash glad slop
          last home ring next road
          feed wean fire this shop
          that bead poke soft tear
          push risk wipe blub hoop
          rash clap skip lull sing
          skin doll girl lift song
          ears boys slip star trip
          moon park rain roof boat
          fist gate ball leaf duck
          step grip sand bite dusk
          take pail dawn gums chum
          wave noon stir fork shoe
          toes gold stop warm blow
          give puss call pony wail
          turn knee slap puke suds
          lean      open      shut
          year      dear      fall
          wrap      rock      down
          good      snap      mine
          week      true      trot
```

bob cobbing   **from: beethoven today**

bob cobbing   from: a movie book

bob cobbing · a love poem

vegetable
vegetable
vepatchle
vepatchle
vepatchle
vegetable
vegetable

marcus patton   vegetable patch

mownumowmownumeⱢlawnumeⱢlawnumeⱢlawn
mownumowmownumeⱢlawnumeⱢlawnumeⱢlawn
mownumowmownumeⱢlawnumeⱢlawnumeⱢlawn
mownumowmownumeⱢlawnumeⱢlawnumeⱢlawn
mownumowmownumeⱢlawnumeⱢlawnumeⱢlawn
mownumowlawnumeⱢlawnumeⱢlawnumeⱢlawn
mownumowlawnumeⱢlawnumeⱢlawnumeⱢlawn
mownumowlawnumeⱢlawnumeⱢlawnumeⱢlawn

marcus patton   **lawnmown**

31

michael gibbs   **proverb (tree poem 4)**

treestreetree
treestreetree
treestreetree
treestreetree
treestreetree
treestreetree
treestreetree
treestreetree
treestreetree
treestreetree
treestreetree
treestreetree
treestreetree
treestreetree
treestreetree
treestreetree
treestreetree
treestreetree
treestreetree
treestreetree
treestreetree
treestreetree
treestreetree
treestreetree
treestreetree

michael gibbs   **avenue**

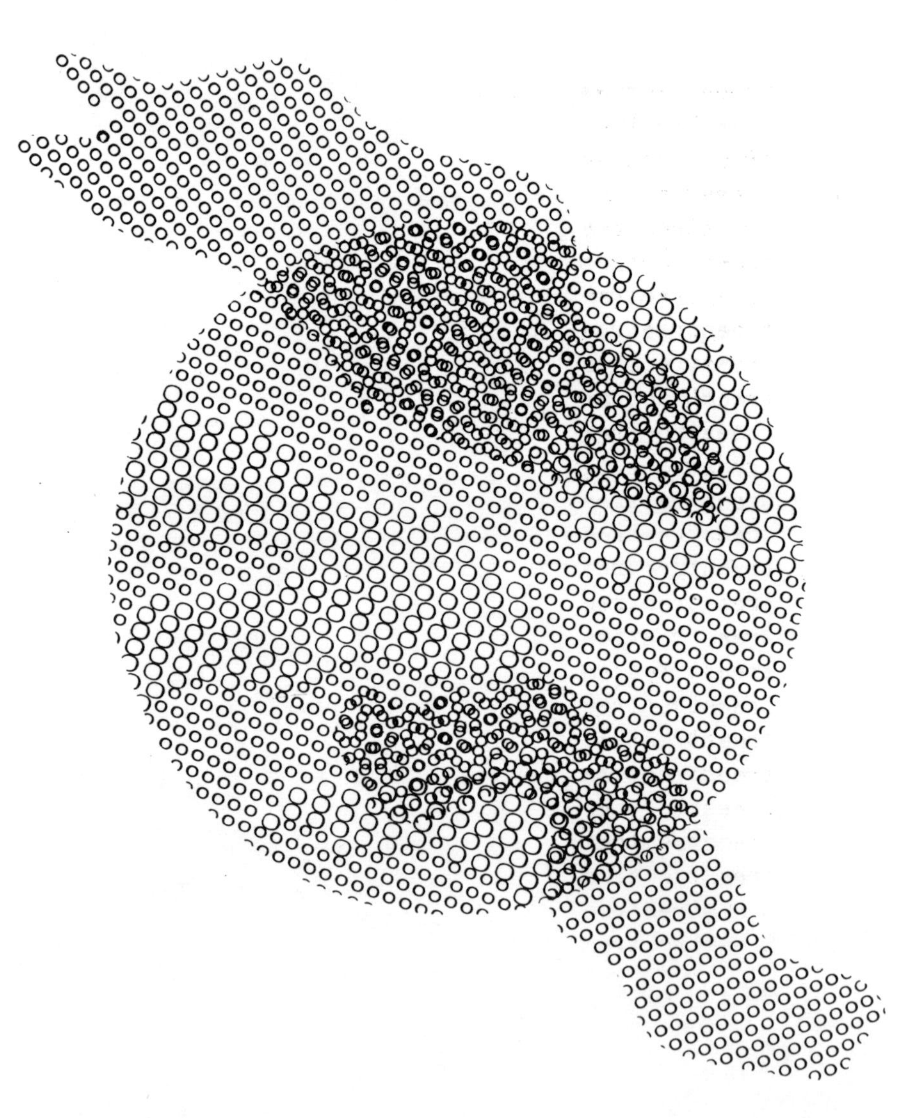

peter finch   texture poem for the moons of stars

34

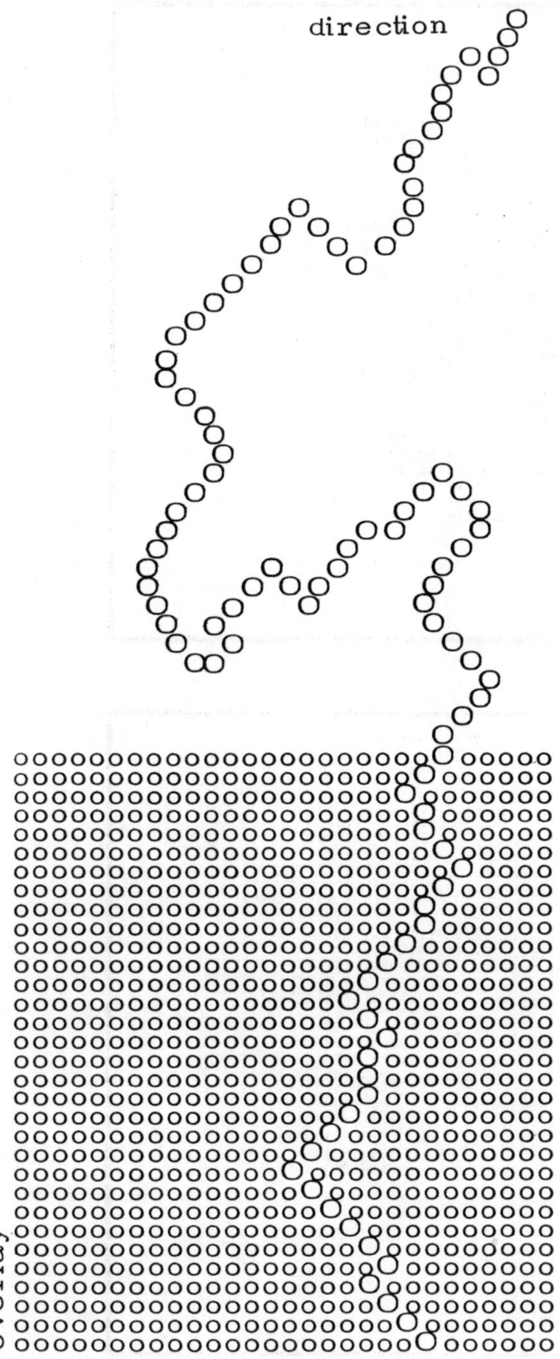

music for
cloud song

peter finch

they whirl
round each other and
where one is the
other is not and
where one is not
the other is in
the heart of the
one that is there
is the one that is
not in the heart of
the one that is not
there is the one that
is they are they are
not they are or are not
they are and are not they
are and are not or are or
are not they   are and
are not and   and are
or are not   they are
they are   not they
are or are   not they
are and are not they are
and are not or are or
are not they are
and are not
and are

                          in
                  the heart
                  of the isn't
                  there is the
                          is

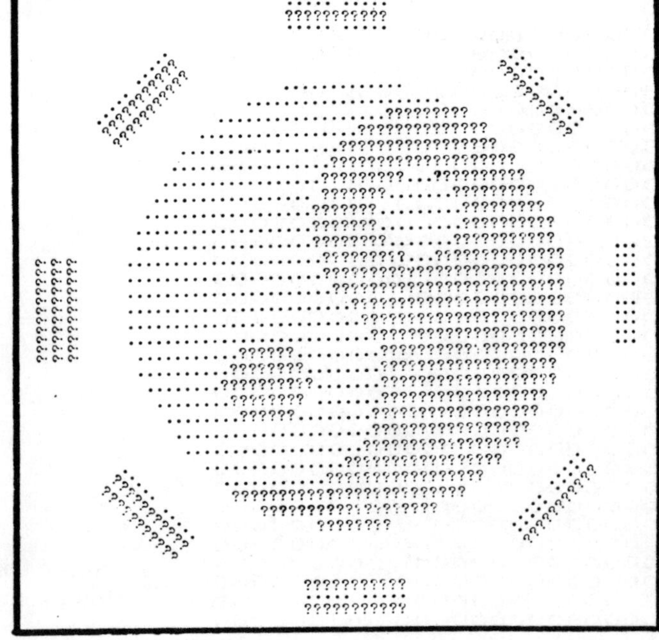

peter mayer

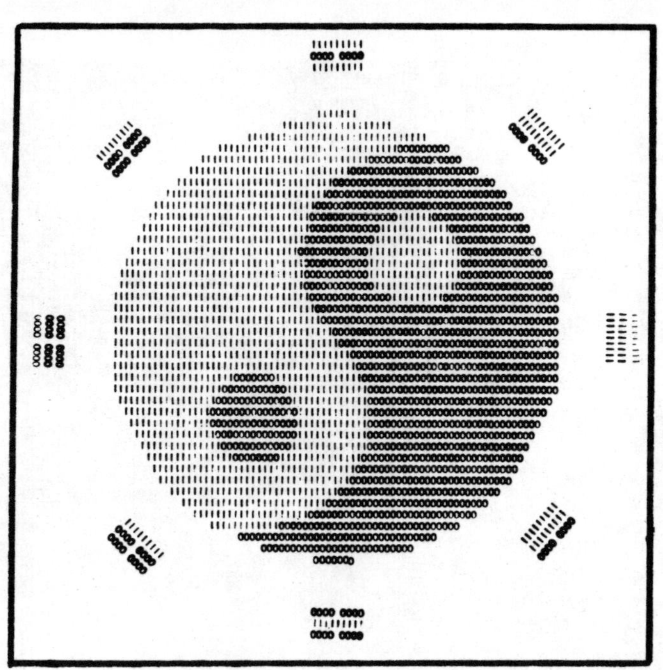

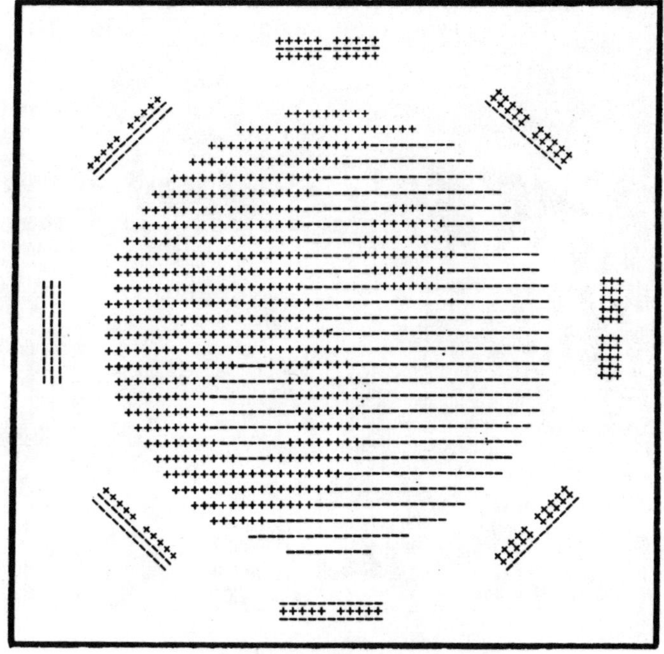

from: the ying yang cube

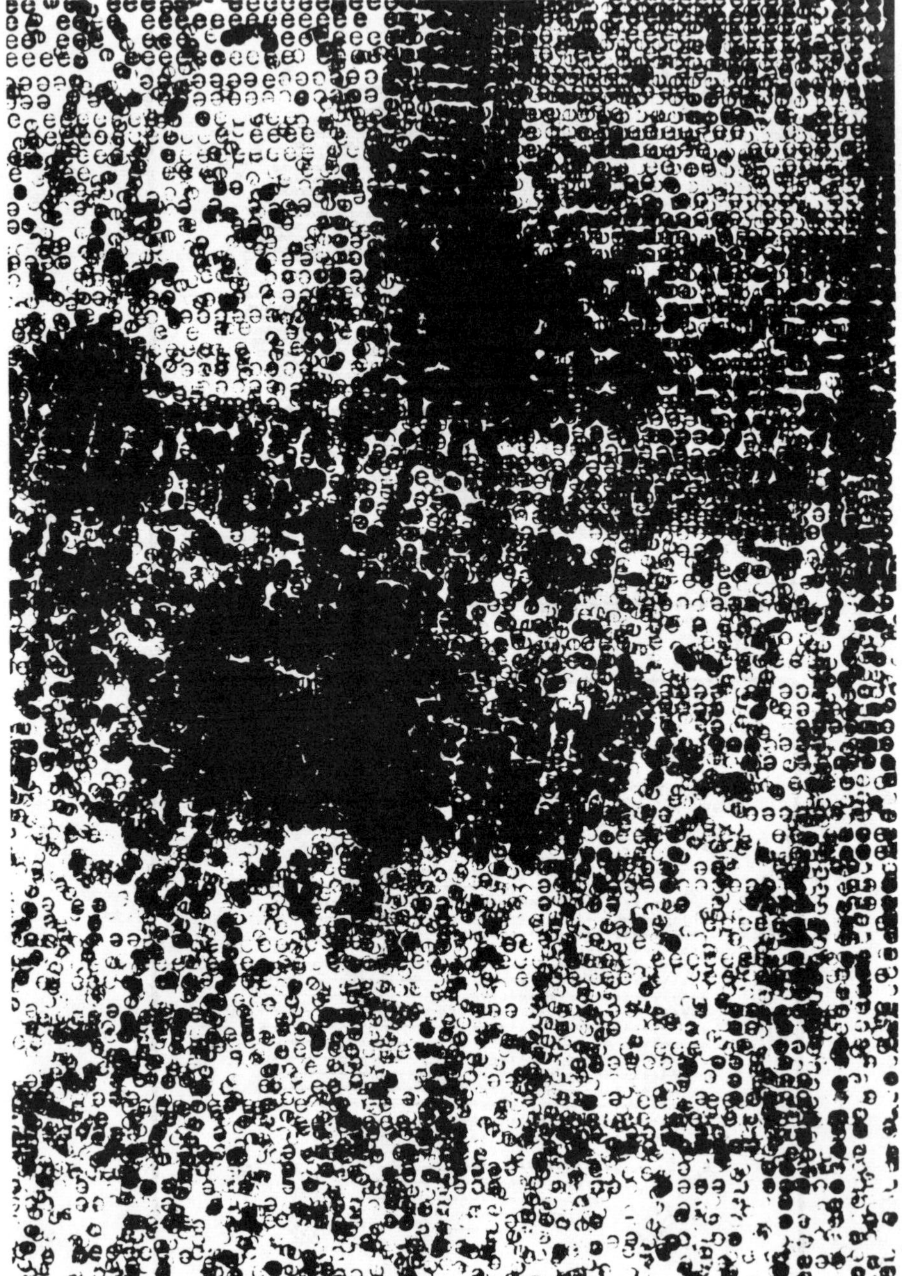

j.p. ward   ease

say urtto you he has ALREADY commit

but i say   he has ALREADY committ
          unto you he has ALREADY committ
b u ti say unto you he   he has ALREADY com
                          he has ALREADY comm
          has ALREADY committed adultery
nto you he has ALREADY committed adultery with her i
                                        with

                              ALRE ADY c
                              A LREADY co

          ou he has ALREADY committe

```
                    t
                h   e   y
            h   i   s   s   s
        a       l   i   t   t   l
    e       b   u   t       k   e   e
p       g   o   o   d       t   i   m   e
a   n   d       m   o   s   t       h   a   v   e
    s   e   v   e   n       h   e   a   d   s
        s   o       t   h   e   y       c
            a   n       s   i   n   g
                c   h   o   r   d
                    r       d   r
                            s
```

```
                    w
                    h
                    e
                n       o
                n   e   g   e
            t   s   i   n       -
        w   h   a   t   i   s       i
    t       l   i   k   e   ?       i   t
    i   s       u   p       a   n   d       d
        o   w   n       a   n   d       t
            h   e       r   o   a   d
                s   t   o   p   s
                    d   i   r
                        e
                        c
                        t
                        l
                        y
```

charles verey

from: some very idle diamonds
reset for john ruskin.

n +
  n   +
    n
  + n
      n +
    + n
         +
         n
        n +
       +
          n +
         + n

==+==n====n====+====+=======n=n======+==+==n=+====+=
+==n===+==+====n===+===+===n=+=+==n==n=+====+=
==n====+===n=n====+=+===n====n====+==+====n==n==+
                    +
                      +
                     +
                     +
                   + + +
                     +

                       +   +

                       +   +
                        +
                          +
                          +
                            +

nicholas zurbrugg   **alphabetpoem**

ffffffffffffffff
ffff ffffffffff
ffff ffffffffff
ffffffffffffffff
ffffffffffffffff
ffffffffffffffff
ffffffffffffffff
fffffffffffffff

cavan mccarthy

f

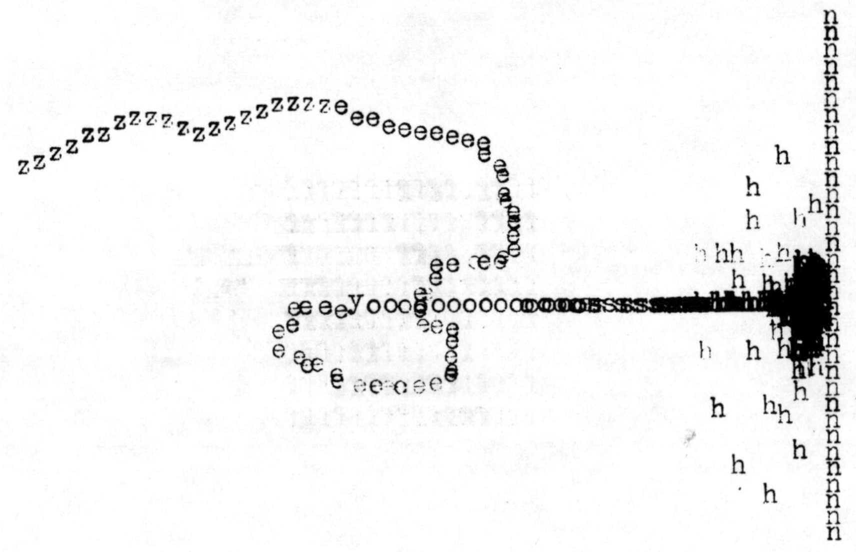

cavan mccarthy

zeeeyooosshhhhhhh

44

notes

alison bielski born newport 1925. author of two books of more
traditional poetry & an experimental set *20 monogrampoems* published
by *writers forum.* currently working on a large series of canvases
which involve image & word. "I resent being tied to a machine,
preferring the freedom of a paintbrush, or varied letter forms. But
every medium presents a challenge opening windows onto new fields."

paula claire works mainly as a sound poet, often with bob cobbing,
and has given performances throughout europe. *"Epithalamion -*
version two of an audience participation poem given its first perform-
ance at the institute of contemporary arts, london, in *'Kroklok'*
february '71. the presentation i would prefer is for this poem to be
printed on a separate sheet of paper, formed into a cylinder so that
the words form a continuous band; the poem should be revolved
in the hands and read/sung by several voices."

thomas a. clark born greenock, scotland 1944. editor (with charles
verey) of *south street publications,* one of the uk's leading exper-
imental publishers.   has now moved away from the concrete move-
ment to a certain extent & believes that his interest in concrete "has
given me a greater appreciation of the value of a word as a thing-
in-itself". his contribution to this anthology first appeared in *some
flame poetry* in the mid-sixties.

bob cobbing born enfield 1920. britain's leading sound poet &
probably the only experimental poet to make a living from his work.
runs *writers forum,* a press dealing with experimental & other
obscure texts. his books include *kurrirrurriri, sonic icons, three
poems for voice and movement,* and many others. his sound poems
have appeared on numerous european radio programs & l.p. records.
"one can get the measure of a poem with the typewriters acurate

left/right & up & down movements; but superimposition by means of
stencil and duplicator enable one to dance to this measure."

peter finch born cardiff 1947. editor of *second aeon,* a magazine
of all poetries. received an arts council bursary for experimental
poetry in 1969. books include *the end of the vision* (jjc ltd), *the
edge of tomorrow* (bb books), *beyond the silence* (vertigo). has
exhibited works at swansea, cardiff, newcastle, university of
california etc. currently working on an experimental novel *thus
has it always been.*

michael gibbs born 1949. editor of *kontexts,* a magazine of exp-
erimental poetry. has exhibited works at buenos aires,   brescia
italy, & a one man show at warwick university in 1970. "dissat-
isfied with tendancy towards typographical decorativeness and
simple typewriter games (have virtually ceased using typewriter
medium) - more interested now in some sort of global/social
relevance - concrete poetry needs to develop but still somehow
remain poetic."

john gilbert born 1948. co-editor of *crab grass,* the best exper-
imental magazine in northern ireland. "likes: armchairs. dislikes:
light blue. a typewriter poem is a right type o'poem."

dom sylvester houedard born guernsey 1924. a monk at prinknash
abbey, gloucester. britains first and leading experimental poet.
publications include *op and kinkon poems and some non-kinkon*
(writers forum) & *dance poems for the cosmic typewriter* (south
street). has exhibited in all the major concrete exhibitions of the
world and has appeared in all major anthologies. "my own type-
stracts are all produced on a portable olivetti lettera 22 (olivetti

himself/themselves show sofar a total non interest in this fact)
there are 86 typeunits available on my machine for use w/2 color
or no ribbon - or with carbons of various colors - the maximum
size surface w/out folding is abt 10" diagonal - the ribbons may
be of various ages - several ribbons may be used on a single
typestract - inked-ribbon & manifold (carbon) can be combined on
same typestract - pressures may be varied - overprints and
semioverprints (½back or ½forward) are available - stencils may
be cut & masks used - precise placing of the typestract units is
possible thru spacebar & ratcheted-roller - or roller may be dis-
engaged &/or spacecontrol disengaged... typestracts - rhythm of
typing - action poetry - as words grow on paper to see language
grow - dictionary (convention as language-coffin - this word/poem
means the WAY we use it - we (not them) convene its meaning-"

philip jenkins "i was born in 1949, pisces w/ cancer ascendant.
i lead a quiet harmless life w/ diverse amusements. i have been
in love 4 times & arrested 3 times. my father is a celebrated
contributor of poems to *the justices of the peace & local govt review*
but my self im not interested in poetry. i assemble, construct,
arrange, compose, design, dismantle & perform a few conjuring
tricks for an encore but i do not consider myself primarily an
entertainer. the sketches included here are from *the fantasy child
hood reset* (second aeon publications, 1971). i'm not prepared
to say anymore at this stage - except i think ive lost the cheque
you sent me." other books by philip jenkins include *the germ
layed deviations* (cunnilingus press 1971)

andrew lloyd born 1943 surrey. books include *the quietest ice*
(vertigo) "a typewriter is a poem. a poem is not a typewriter.
sometimes i have enjoyed dabbing sounds onto paper, growling &

crooning thru the trees i have enjoyed myself more and run less
risk of being taken seriously. once i broke both arms in falling out
of a tree. cavan mccarthy introduced me to typewriter poetry.
when a sceptic told him an ape let loose on a typewriter could
produce work as good as his, cavan replied that this was the
beauty of it all. after his wedding, cavan gave me a branding iron
stamped with my initials. he has taken to making jewelry and will
depart for south america soon. during the week of the cuban missile
crisis, i was fatuous enough to lie on the steps of the american
embassy, any siren, any passing aeroplane filled us with appre-
hension. big words:— (1) a global destruction *was* imminent (read
the books). (2) it was seen to be imminent. (3) a global insur-
rection was absent... 3 is most fuckawful thing that i know. nothing
i write will have the significance of that one fatuous act we made.
i am not being a nihilist; i am not being original; i am not boasting
my humanity. i am writing a note on typewriter poetry. notes on
tidal poem: 1. this is a typewriter poem. 2. i thought to make it a
sound poem. imagine a heavy gilt picture frame containing a grid
of indistinguishable pressure pads; each pad can activate a (letter)
sound stored on a small loop of tape & played from the stereo head
phones that hang from the frame. imagine a gallery of these pictures
that can be explored by the audience preferably with their eyes
closed. the tidal poem and others. participation? - personally, i'd
get more from learning to play the penny whistle. 3. i also thought
to make it an environmental poem. i would acquire hundreds of
buoys, mark each with a letter of the poem, write it in the sea
and watch it re-form and disintegrate with the tide. a most expen-
sive poem. i prefer to watch the sea. this is not a typewriter
poem. these are sounds in space, these are words at sea. each
letter forms in myriad intonations. perceive it thus. or how you
will.

peter mayer editor of *verb publications.* a scholar in classical chinese & a chinese calligrapher. his works, often 3-D visual items, have appeared in such places as *oz, it, running man, poetry review, etc.* currently doing the rounds with an illustrated lecture *3000 years of visual poetry.*

cavan mccarthy born bristol 1943. editor of the uk's longest lived experimental magazine *tlaloc,* one man exhibition of typestracts at bristol arts centre. "i have never published a separate book of verse, apart from an exhibition catalogue, and have never made an unsolicited contribution of poetry to a magazine" now moving even further away, devoting his energies to the manufacture of small concrete poems embeded in jewelry.

edwin morgan born glasgow 1920. fully at home and well respected with both traditional and experimental verse forms. included in most major concrete anthologies and exhibited widely. books include *penguin modern poets 15, emergent poems* (hansjord mayer), *starryveldt* (gomringer press), *proverbfolder* (openings press) and many others. "typewriter poems are hard to define, but i would call this one because only on a typewriter can you get the 4-letter words all coming out even and forming to overall pattern. (eg when this poem was printed in *unit* the lines came out all ragged, since a typewriter was not used, and the whole effect was ruined.)

will parfitt born cheltenham 1950, currently at nottingham. editor of *vertigo publications.* books include *an afternoon of eyes* (quickest way out) *midnight on the diamond air* (second aeon) & *poem for cavan* (cunnilingus press)

marcus patton born 1948. co-editor of *crab grass* where his contributions here first appeared. likes: asparagus. dislikes: dis-

liking. "wants a poem to say something unimportant as briefly and
interestingly as possible."

l.d. pedersen editor of the *helleborine pancarte* series of prints,
texts, etc. "typewriter arabesques...i am not sure if this neo-
concrete genre is infact relevant.........i find the most reason for
these is not the geometric shape (ie the concreteness) but rather
the sound poem inherent."

alan riddell born queensland 1927. moved to the uk 1938. founder
of the review *lines.* numerous books of non-visual poetry published.
has exhibited visual texts at buenos aires, stedelijk museum holland,
royal festival hall, etc. one man show at the 57 gallery, edinburgh.
a collection of his visual work *eclipse* will be published by calder
& boyars in 1972.

john j. sharkey born in dublin 1936, editor of *structure,* a mag-
azine of environmental art, made a poem-film *openwordrobe* in 1964
and now working on another. has just edited an anthology of
concrete poetry for the lorrimer press. ". . .(an half-moon for james
joyce, '64) oscillates between the title (on the bottom of the page)
& the poem itself, each acting as a complement to the other within
the total visual shape - the joycean content, elaborated upon a
central axis, is retained even with my final interrogative 'na', a
gaelic negative participle."

meic stephens born pontypridd 1938. editor of *poetry wales* and
is assistant director for literature with the welsh arts council. books
include *triad* (triskel press). "My po(l)em *osmosis* is an attempt
to describe how the political and linguistic aspirations of Welsh
nationality are related. The text 'genesis' consists of a quotation

from the Gospel according to John (Chapter 1, verse 1), from
the Bible in Welsh ("In the beginning was the Word"). It is meant
to convey graphically Man's first attempt at speech. The phrase
also has a secondary significance which, for me, is more import
ant. It was the first phrase I learned, but couldn't understand, for
recitation in the Sunday School when I was a child. I have learned
to speak Welsh as an adult and owe much of my interest to the
experience of those early years."

charles verey born gloucester 1940. editor of *south street public-
ations.* has exhibited and published work widely. books include
loom songs (south street) *re a vow al* (writers forum) & *news
from the south* (second aeon) from which his contribution here is
taken.

j.p. ward lecturer in english at swansea university. has been
responsible for organizing two exhibitions of concrete poetry in wales,
at the university swansea, and the arts council gallery cardiff.
books include *the other man* (christopher davies) and a forthcoming
set from second aeon. "To me a typewriter poem must, necessarily,
be that which could only have been done with a typewriter, and not
with hand-writing, print, or caligraphic manuscript. The type-
writer, unlike all those things, is a grid system, with each space
of equivalent size. It goes across and down, one space at a time,
and is best used that way. One can, admittedly, do that with hand
writing and print, as indeed one can pull a piece of typing paper
all ways at once in the machine, but neither extreme captures the
respective medium's recognizable qualities, because neither comes
naturally. So the type-writer lends itself to geometry, abstraction,
and therefore, perhaps, to the infinite, the deep truth that 'number
holds sway above the flux'. Sadly we all too often reduce this to

the level of typing pretty patterns of very elementary nature, and
feel pleased with ourselves for doing so, but more elaborate
patterns, including semantic ones, of greater intricacy and intelli-
gence are possible - requiring only the poets with the patience to
find them."

nicholas zurbrugg texts exhibited in uk, france, italy, argentina,
canada, etc. "editor/publisher of *stereo headphones,* an occas-
ional review documenting the new poetries... issues 1&2/3 sold
out - sonic issue 4 @25p with cobbing, chopin, hausmann, nichol,
jandl, de vree, heidsiek, etc etc from stereo headphones, church
steps, kersey, near ipswich - well plugs ARE necessary.......
visual punctuation of visual poetry perhaps best allows symmetric-
ally ordered presentations of kinetic poly-semantic statements of
the semantic/visual ambiguities that obsess me. i like simplicity,
movement, ambiguity. i like the art of soto, of barnett newmann.
i'd like to meet the man who put the leaves on trees on ends
of branches."

acknowledgements for some of the poems that appear in this
collection are due to the following:

*ambit, some flame poetry, crab grass, exit, writers forum, second
aeon publications, unit, her(m)etic press, and poetry wales.*